Go where the PEACE IS

BRAVEGIRLS Club

MELODY ROSS

Andrews McMeel
Publishing®
a division of Andrews McMeel Universal

Sometimes to find peace, we have to make really tough choices that don't feel comfortable, but feel right and true.

Living a peaceful life often requires *this kind of bravery...*

It is hard to feel at peace when

you are at war with yourself.

You've got to 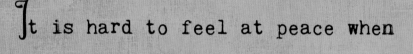be your own ally;

you've got to be on your own side.

Make a truce and

build a friendship

with the beautiful soul

that you are.

Peace starts

in your heart,

in your thoughts.

You can't look outside

of yourself to find

the peace that needs

to live inside of you.

You've got to

go deep to find peace,

deep inside

of yourself.

Step into this day, into this year, into this age of your life. Don't waste it by wishing for a different set of circumstances.

Embrace, accept,

and *do your best*

with the absolute.

Make peace
with what
cannot be changed.

Choose
What Matters

Every day, look around and ask yourself what matters most to you...no matter what else is on *your list.*

Arrange your life around what is precious, instead of giving it only your leftover time.

Peace comes

when you choose

what matters most.

When you have expectations

of others, those expectations often

end in disappointment and resentment.

It is not fair to make others

responsible for your happiness, and

it is hard to feel at peace when

you give that control to someone else.

Realize that everyone

is doing their best,

and take your life back

into your own hands.

Feel the peace

that comes from

letting others off the hook.

Always be the one
who tells your truth before
someone else can tell
their own version of it.
Be true to your word.
Tell the whole story.

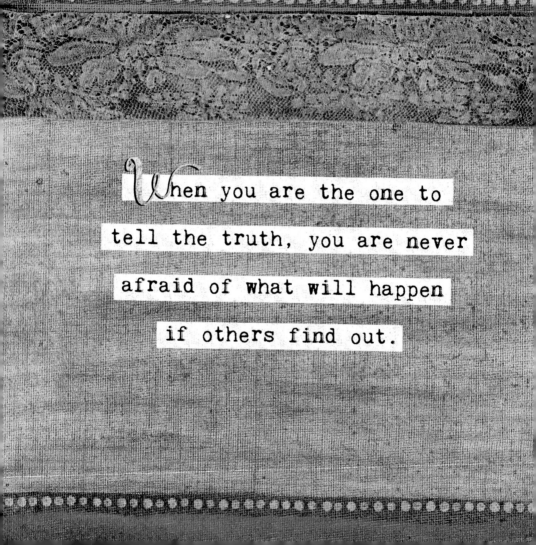

When you are the one to tell the truth, you are never afraid of what will happen if others find out.

The truth is

where the peace is.

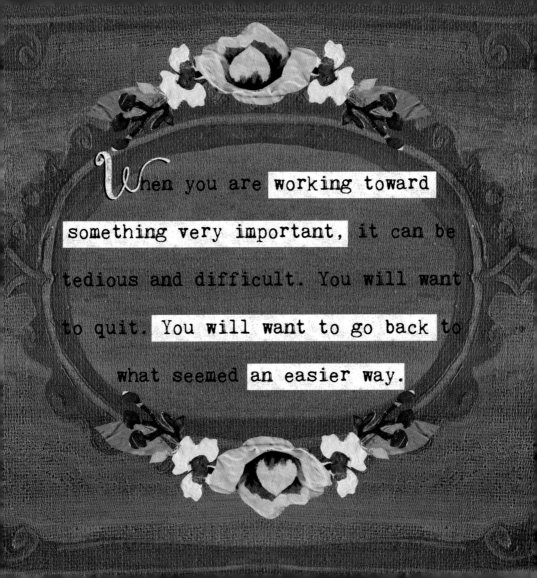

When you are working toward something very important, it can be tedious and difficult. You will want to quit. You will want to go back to what seemed an easier way.

These are the times
when it is **most important** to
remember why you started.

Peace comes

when we choose

to stay with it.

No Good &
Bad Piles

What if there wasn't a good pile or a bad pile? What if we all just gave each other a lifetime grace card? What if we approach life KNOWING that everyone is going to make some big mistakes and that when they do, they aren't automatically going to get thrown out to the trash pile?

When we give others *a grace card,* we give ourselves one too.

No more

good and bad piles.

Only peace.

In a world that is noisy to
our minds and noisy to our
hearts and noisy to our souls...
it is hard to find quiet.
It is hard to find answers...
it is hard to find peace.

But dear friend,

it is worth the work

it takes to

quiet everything,

Because all of

the answers will

be found in

the stillness.

Going and going and going
and doing and doing and doing
leaves no time for peace,
especially when you keep moving
so that you do not
have to feel your life.

Make time to really feel, to really see, to really hear.

Peace comes
when you bravely
slow down.

Beautiful friend, don't assume that others know what you mean or what you want. Try not to speak in hints, hoping that others will fill in the blanks.

Be clear and loving
in your communication.

Say what
you mean,
and feel at peace.

*P*eace comes when you decide what

you will do and what you

will not do, when there are

clear boundaries.

Make boundaries

that keep the good things

protected and the

bad things out.

Draw a clear line

and make it known.

When your heart tells you
that there is a need, and that you
could help with that need...you will
feel so much more peaceful if you step
in and do something about it.

Helping others,

especially the weak

and the unprotected,

is the right thing to do.

When someone needs help

please don't look away.

Things can happen in life that knock you to your knees, and sometimes it is hard to recover. When you hold on to bitterness, you cannot feel peace.

You can choose to *let things go,* to move forward with a clean slate.

Avoid Drama

You can avoid drama by refusing to participate in gossip, owning your part in every situation, sticking to the facts, and taking the emotion out of interactions with others.

Avoiding drama
creates a
peaceful environment
and
protects your peace.

Choose to *walk away* from drama.

You have to eliminate the things that take the peace away...the background noise, the hustling and bustling, the opinions, the who and how you are supposed to be.

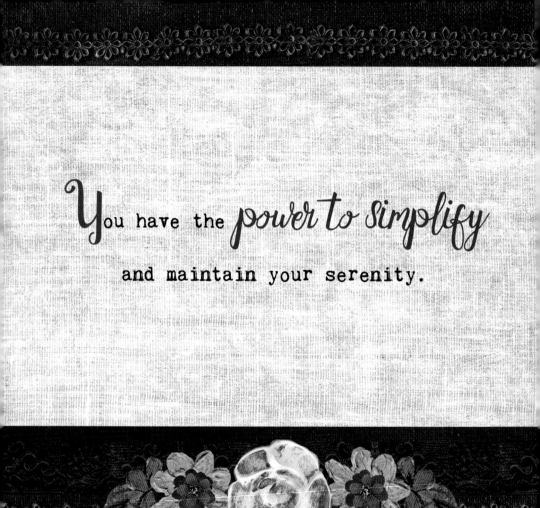

You have the *power to simplify* and maintain your serenity.

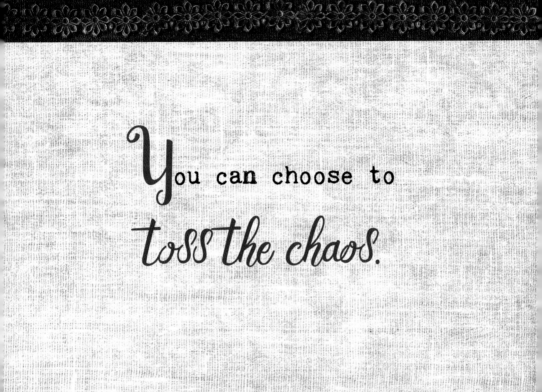

You can choose to
toss the chaos.

It is easy to keep your thoughts in the future, worrying about what is to come, or in the past, worrying about making it right. Nothing matters more in this moment than this moment.

You can be in this moment,
seeing who and what is in
your life now, being part of
what is happening today.

Choose to be here now,

where the peace is.

Today, just make the solid decision that you will do whatever it takes to feel peace for the rest of the day. When a difficult feeling or situation arises, remind yourself of the commitment that you made.

Focus your mind on the beauty of the world, on the love that others have for you, on the love that you have for others, and on the blessings that you find in the moment.

Peace can be right here. Right now.

Choose Peace.

Andrews McMeel Publishing
a division of Andrews McMeel Universal
1130 Walnut Street, Kansas City, Missouri 64106

www.andrewsmcmeel.com
bravegirlsclub.com

16 17 18 19 20 TEN 10 9 8 7 6 5 4 3 2 1

ISBN: 978-1-4494-6728-9

Library of Congress Control Number: 2015955100

ATTENTION SCHOOLS & BUSINESSES
Andrews McMeel books are available at quantity
discounts with bulk purchase for educational,
business, or sales promotional use. For information,
please email the Andrews McMeel Publishing Special
Sales Department: specialsales@amuniversal.com.